The Throne Room
Experience

The Throne Room Experience

*

The Dynamics of True Worship

Calvin L. Lewis & Roderick L. Evans

Kingdom Builders
PUBLISHING
CAMDEN, NORTH CAROLINA

The Throne Room Experience
The Dynamics of True Worship

All Rights Reserved. Copyright © 2011 Calvin L. Lewis &
Roderick L. Evans

**Unless otherwise indicated, all of the scripture quotations are
taken from the** *Authorized King James Version* **of the Bible.
Scripture quotations marked with NIV are taken from the** *New
International Version* **of the Bible. Scripture quotations marked
with NASV are taken from the** *New American Standard Version*
**of the Bible. Scripture quotations marked with Amplified are
taken from the** *Amplified Bible*.

978-1-60141-194-5

Printed in the United States of America

Contents

No Flesh Should Glory in His Presence

I can remember being in a service. The music was playing and the Praise and Worship team was singing with uplifted voices. Everybody seemed to be enjoying the service. However, no matter how hard I tried, I just could not get into the service. I started clapping my hands, singing, I even stood up. The more involved I became, the more out of place I felt. I somewhat felt like Job.

> *Behold, I go forward, but he is not there; and backward, but I cannot perceive him. Job 23:8 (KJV)*

At that point, I started questioning myself, thinking that something was wrong with me. I started praying that God would remove from me whatever was separating me from the service. I asked Him to open my heart so that I could receive, open my spiritual eyes so that I could see, and my spiritual ears so that I could hear. It was to my surprise that when the Holy Spirit opened my eyes, ears and heart, I was not ready for what I saw, heard, or felt.

Strange Fire

The music had no form or rhythm, the words to the song had no meaning it was just a bunch of noise. All of the mechanics of music ministry were in place, but there was no real sense of God's presence. It reminded me of Aaron's sons.

> *And Nadab and Abihu, the sons of Aaron, took either of them his censer, and put fire therein, and put incense thereon, and offered strange fire before the Lord, which he commanded them not. Lev 10:1 (KJV)*

They went in to offer sacrifice, but it was not how God commanded it to be offered. The same was happening before my eyes. Praise and worship was being offered, but it was not something that God received at the time. I do believe that God was allowing me to see, hear, and feel as He did for that moment.

Consequently, I completely understood what I was feeling. I was able to participate physically, but my spirit was not agreeing with what was taking place. So many times, we participate in praise and worship and do not quite get anything out of it. Simply put, it is because there is too much flesh involved. Strange fire of praise and worship is being offered before the Lord. We must return to offering sacrifices of praise and thanksgiving with a pure heart and motive; that is, with a focus to exalt, magnify, and glorify our God.

Command Versus Beg

The scriptures are clear that God deserves and expects praise and worship from His people. It is not a denominational concept to praise and worship God; it is the legacy of the servants of God in Both Testaments. Therefore, God commands us to praise and worship, but He will never beg! Have you ever been in a service where the praise and worship leaders exhaust themselves trying to get the people to praise God? As a former praise and worship leader, I can remember spending a lot time trying to encourage and provoke the people to join in the worship and praise of God.

Rather than being refreshed and leading the people into worship, I was exhausted trying to get others to praise and worship Him. However, those who lead worship and those who participate in praise and worship ought to come into the place of worship praising God. Let us remember the exhortations and commands of the scripture.

> *O come, let us sing unto the Lord: let us make a joyful noise to the rock of our salvation. Psalms 95:1 (KJV)*
>
> *Praise ye the Lord: for it is good to sing praises unto our God; for it is pleasant; and praise is comely. Psalms 147:1 (KJV)*

The scriptures demonstrate that praise and worship are the responsibility of the believer at the command of God. We ought to have praise in our heart, continually. WE HAVE SO MUCH TO BE THANKFUL FOR.

David is a prime example of a how God's people should live in praise. He offers an excellent example of what true praise is. He made the statement "I will bless the Lord at all times: his praise shall always be in my mouth (Psalm 34:1)." This leads us to believe that David was always willing to praise God, no matter what the situation or circumstance. It did not even mater to David who was standing around. There was an account when David danced out of his clothes.

> *And as the ark of the Lord came into the city of David, Michal Saul's daughter looked through a window, and saw king David leaping and dancing before the Lord. 2 Sam 6:16 (KJV)*

David's status of king did not stop him from dancing with abandon before the Lord until his outer garments came off. He understood that his praise of God has to match God's greatness. God does not beg us, but command us to praise. The person who will lead worship and those involved must remember this truth.

Courts of Praise and Worship

In the Old Testament, the Tabernacle had three main areas connected to the sacrificial system. There was the outer court, the inner court, and the holiest of all. In looking at these three, we discover some truths concerning the dynamic of worship. Those involved in worship ministry will be able to identify with these.

Outer Court Praise & Worship

The outer court was the where any Israelite could enter desiring to make a sacrifice. This is where the praise and worship of many churches is. This is demonstrated when individuals who lead worship and those who participate go through the mechanics of worship without entering into the Lord's presence. The music sounds good, the singing is great, there is a good feeling, and people seem to be in worship. However, they remain on the outer courts, not worshipping the Lord in the beauty of holiness.

Rather, the praise and worship comes from stylistic and musical religiosity, not from a passionate relationship with Him. Hence, there is a lot of flesh involved. Where flesh and human skill are on display, true praise and worship is absent. The act of praise and worship occurs without the proper attitude and approach to praise and worship.

Inner Court Praise & Worship

The inner court was reserved only for priests. This is the place where the daily sacrifices were offered to the Lord. It was the adjacent to the holies of all. It reflected a closer proximity to the Lord's abiding presence. Some churches have entered into this place.

As sacrifices were made in the inner court, so many, have understood that they must cleanse themselves (offering their bodies as a living sacrifice) to prepare to have a genuine praise and worship experience. Praise and worship in this area is characterized by the presence of God, however, inner transformation and change is absent during these times.

Holy Place Praise & Worship

The final area of the Tabernacle was the holiest of all, called the Holy Place. It is where the mercy seat and cherubim were. It is the place where the tangible presence of God was said to abide. When praise and worship goes into this place, it will not be mechanical. It will not be just a good feeling and time.

It will be a time of repentance and refreshing in the presence of the Lord. It will be characterized by His name and holiness being magnified and exalted in the earth. This is the true definition of the throne room experience in praise and worship. In this atmosphere, no flesh is able or desires to glory in His presence. It should be the desire of every worship leader to being people into this holy place, rather than try to lead the people to themselves. In the chapters to follow, we will examine the dynamics of true worship, which is the foundation for having a throne room experience. It is time for no flesh to glory in His presence, but that His name is exalted in the churches.

Chapter 1	# The Worship Established

What is worship? It is a word that is commonly used. However, many do not understand the implications of what it means to worship. A throne room experience in worship brings us into the tangible presence of the Lord. However, to enter in, we must have a proper understanding of worship.

The Definition of Worship

Jesus stated that those who worship God must worship Him in spirit and in truth. Worship is an outward demonstration of an inner conviction and relationship with God. Thus, the heart of worship does not begin with religious adulation bestowed upon God. It begins with the lifestyle of those who serve Him. To understand worship, we want to look at three factors concerning it.

1. Worship is Sacrifice. The worship of God finds its roots in sacrifice. Abraham was willing to sacrifice someone that was dear to him in order to worship. He described the potential sacrifice of his son as worship. If we want to enter into true worship, we have to have this mindset. I will enter into His presence, even if it costs me.

> *And Abraham said unto his young men, Abide ye here with the ass; and I and the lad will go yonder and worship, and come again to you. (Genesis 22:5)*

Before we can enter into God's presence fully via worship, we have to willing to give up everything first. If we are to experience true worship, our love for God has to supersede our love of anyone and anything else.

2. Worship is Subsistence. Worship is to characterize the believer's life and existence. The believer is worship. It is to be his condition or state of being. The believer recognizes that it is through the Lord that he exists and does all things.

> *Whether therefore ye eat, or drink, or whatsoever ye do, do all to the glory of God. Give none offence, neither to the Jews, nor to the Gentiles, nor to the church of God. (I Corinthians 10:31-32)*

His life should be a living demonstration of worship. While eating, sleeping, working, and relaxing, the Lord's glory and honor should not be diminished. Our daily activities should bring glory and not offence to God. Our lives are to be subject to His righteousness.

3. Worship is Selfless. Worship is not designed for man, but it is reserved for God alone. There is a tendency (especially seen among Pentecostal and Charismatic Christians) to believe worship is for their benefit. Though worship blesses believers, its sole purpose is to exalt and magnify the personality and power of the true and living God. Isaiah prophetically reveals this truth,

> *I am the Lord: that is my name: and my glory will I not give to another, neither my praise to graven images. (Isaiah 42:8)*

The Christian is to worship in appreciation and honor of God. He is not to worship with the selfish motive of receiving a blessing. God blesses us daily. Therefore, believers should regard the opportunity to worship God as a privilege. This is because only His people are able to approach Him in worship. Remember, worship is built upon three truths: it is sacrifice, it is subsistence, and it is selfless. Without these, there will be no throne room experience, only a religious exercise rather than communion with God. Though there are many ways to worship, we want to look at the act of worship. How do we visibly worship God during the praise and worship experience.

The Demonstration of Worship

What does it mean to worship? How do we act it out? We now look at the demonstration of worship. In the scriptures, there are numerous meanings to the word we find translated worship. When we understand these, we will be able to offer up to God true worship, having a throne room experience.

> *O come, let us worship and bow down: let us kneel before the Lord our maker. (Psalm 95:6)*

True worship comes from the knowledge that God is Supreme and the Creator of all things. He possesses all wisdom, power, and authority. Worship means to bow down or to prostrate before His greatness. Therefore, when we say we worship God, there ought to be some actions that follow. Whether in the religious setting or in the personal lives of believers, worship requires more than a verbal declaration.

When we say that we worship God, we have to demonstrate what we are saying. If not, then our declarations are only empty words. We have to refrain from hypocrisy. We sing songs and hymns which convey the intent to worship. The only thing that is lacking is following through. Jesus warned against this type of worship when He exposed the vain worship of the people in His day.

> *This people draweth nigh unto me with their mouth, and honoureth me with their lips; but their heart is far from me. But in vain they do worship me… (Matthew 15:8-9a)*

Our words of worship should never be vain sayings. The words of our mouths should match the intention of our hearts. We have stated that to worship means to bow down or to prostrate.

How does this occur in the religious setting? When we speak of religious setting, we mean corporate or personal settings set aside for the overall worship and reverence of God. Again, how is worship to be demonstrated after we have declared our intent through word or song?

Bowing of the Head

Regardless of the setting, when one wants to demonstrate worship, he may bow his head in reverence to God. When the head is bowed, it symbolizes that our thoughts are turned toward Him. We submit our ways unto His and our thoughts unto His because God's ways and thoughts are higher than ours.

> *For my thoughts are not your thoughts, neither are your ways my ways, saith the Lord. For as the heavens are higher than the earth, so are my ways higher than your ways, and my thoughts than your thoughts. (Isaiah 55:8-9)*

The bowing of the head demonstrates submission unto God's purposes. It reflects our intention to submit or bow to His wisdom and word. In services, we bow our heads oftentimes when prayers are made. If we do this, we are telling the Lord that we bow our wills to His in response to our requests.

Bowing at the Waist

Depending upon the religious setting, some may feel at liberty to bow unto the Lord while in a standing position (accompanied with the lifting of hands). This type of bowing demonstrates reverence for His greatness. This type of bowing is done in respect to God as the One who fills heaven and earth.

> ***Thus saith the Lord, The heaven is my throne, and the earth is my footstool… (Isaiah 66:1)***

In Asian culture, it is customary to bow when meeting acquaintances and respecting those in authority. In the Church, we are friends and servants of God. We bow to show personal intimacy and respect.

Bowing at the waist also represents that we set our personal desires aside to honor the Lord. This is why usually during corporate worship and personal times of devotion we do not eat, drink, and meet other physical needs to give Him our undivided attention. Everything we have is to be submitted to Him in the act of worship. It also demonstrates that while we are in worship, we will submit any ungodly desires and appetites of the flesh unto the Lord.

> ***Having therefore these promises, dearly beloved, let us cleanse ourselves from all filthiness of the flesh and spirit, perfecting holiness in the fear of God. (II Corinthians 7:1)***

True worship will bring men and women into greater levels of personal holiness. Worship helps us to perfect holiness in the fear of the Lord.

Bending of the Knee(s)

Another common demonstration of worship is to kneel before God. Again, this is oftentimes done in connection to prayer. When possible, it should be incorporated into the worship setting. Since it involves the legs, kneeling denotes submission to God's ways. It expresses a willingness to go where He wants you to go. Your volition will be governed by His word.

> *The steps of a good man are ordered by the Lord: and he delighteth in his way. (Psalm 37:23)*

When we kneel in the worship setting, we declare God's supremacy. We demonstrate that He alone stands in control of our lives. We submit the course and direction of our lives unto Him. We kneel to demonstrate that He is above us in authority and power.

Prostrating the Body

One of the greatest expressions of worship in the religious setting is prostration. When one prostrates, he/she is on bended knees with the face to the ground or laid out (usually face down) during the time of worship. This act of worship denotes total surrender to the Lord. Prostration reflects a willingness to submit one's total being unto the Lord. When we do this, we declare our total trust, submission, surrender, and love.

> *Jesus said unto him, Thou shalt love the Lord thy God with all thy heart, and with all thy soul, and with all thy mind. (Matthew 23:27)*

Those that will lay prostrate before Him in worship have to understand that this is what they are communicating. God is in control. No other will be placed before Him. His word is law. His will is unchanging. If we are going to act this out in the worship setting, then we must be prepared to follow through. If not, we become vain worshippers.

How many times have we sang the song, "I Surrender All" in the worship setting? Yet, our lives do not reflect the sentiments of this song. We do not have to be perfect to sing the words to this song. However, if we are to sing it, we should be striving daily to make it a reality in our lives. Songs like this should be meaningful outside of the religious settings.

When we understand what is worship and how to demonstrate worship, we prepare ourselves to enter into true worship in the praise and worship setting. Though we have established what worship is, we must look at the roots of worship and vulnerabilities that come along with worship by examining the pitfalls associated with worship.

| Chapter 2 |

The Worship Expelled

God, in heaven, established worship. Both Testaments agree that one of the major functions of the angelic hosts is to worship God. However simple this truth is, it needs to be stated because many feel that worship is a man-made invention designed to boost the religious experience. However, God instituted praise and worship because He is the creator and source of all things. He should be reverenced and extolled highly.

The Worship Contaminated

The worship of God in heaven was pure. The angels each exalted God and served Him truly in the beauty of holiness. However, one of the guardian cherubs wanted to be worshipped as God, contaminating worship in heaven. We know him as that old serpent, the devil who is called the adversary, Lucifer. Let us look at his story.

The devil's God-given name at his creation was Lucifer. Lucifer means "shining star or son of the morning." God created him as one of His archangels. The book of Ezekiel describes the beauty and honor bestowed upon Lucifer.

You were the model of perfection, full of wisdom and perfect in beauty. You were in Eden, the garden of God. Every precious stone adorned you: ruby, topaz and emerald, chrysolite, onyx and jasper, sapphire, urquoise and beryl. Your settings and mountings were made of gold; on the day you were created, they were prepared. You were anointed as a guardian cherub, for so I ordained you. You were on the holy mount of God and you walked among the fiery stones. You were blameless in your ways from the day you were created... (Ezekiel 28:12-15a NIV)

God made Lucifer perfect. He was anointed to stand by God and walk around the throne of God. He was a guardian cherub around the throne. He was full of wisdom and the perfection of beauty. He was one of God's chief angels and creation. No other angels in the scripture are given such an awesome description, not even Michael or Gabriel.

God's anointing rested upon Lucifer and God had ordained it so. Lucifer was also present at creation for the text says he was in Eden, not as a serpent, but as the anointed cherub of God.

When we consider all that God had bestowed upon him, it is hard to believe that this is the one, whom we now call our adversary. Worship leaders that emulate his actions may become adversaries of God as well. What led to his fall? He stumbled because of his form. What caused the perfect, beautiful, and wise angel to become a fool? What led to his disaster and ruin? How did he go from a wonder to a blunder?

Lucifer had it all. He was perfect in all of his ways, but he fell. Further reading of Ezekiel gives us insight into what caused his fall.

You were blameless in your ways, from the day you were created, till wickedness was found in you. Through your widespread trade, you were filled with violence, and you sinned. So, I drove you out in disgrace from the mount of God, and I expelled thee, O guardian cherub, from among the fiery stones. Your heart became proud on account of your beauty, and you corrupted your wisdom because of your splendor. (Ezekiel 28:15-17a)

Lucifer fell because of pride. He became puffed up because of his beauty. He became infatuated with himself and he "forgot" that he was only a creation. This is why Ezekiel said that his wisdom was corrupted.

Even though he understood he was only a creation of God, his splendor made him arrogant. The wisdom that God had given him was corrupted through pride. His thinking became warped and he began to worship his own beauty and splendor. The worship leader and worshiper must not idolize the method and manner of worship. They must remember it is designed for God alone.

He thought that he should be God. He even caused other angels to rebel against God and follow him. The worship leader must guard against this same type of rebellion. Even those who participate in worship should not become obsessed with how they worship God, trying to gain attention for themselves rather than honor to His name.

The Worship Contained

Lucifer's plan was to take over. He had a list of things that he would do. We see these listed in (Isaiah 14:12-14. However, God would purge heaven and ensure that the worship before His throne remains pure.

> *How art thou fallen from heaven, O Lucifer, son of the morning! How art thou cut to the ground, which didst weak the nations! For thou hast said in thine heart, "I will ascend to heaven, I will exalt my throne above the stars of God, I will sit also upon the mount of the congregation in the sides of the north, I will ascend above the heights of the clouds, and I will be like the most High."*

He actually accomplished the first two. He already was present in heaven. Secondly, when he stated that he would exalt his throne above the stars of God, he meant he would exercise authority over the angels (stars) of God. He succeeded only in part because not all of the angels shared in his delusion.

Satan allowed his beauty, perfection, and wisdom to cloud his judgment. He thought that he could overthrow God. This was his calamity or ruin. He deceived himself.

This should serve as a warning to worship leaders to be aware of pride. God has gifted many to sing and play, to usher people into His service. Worship leaders must not allow the music ministry that God has blessed them with to blind and corrupt them, or they will find themselves walking in the way of Lucifer.

From the passage in Isaiah, we see that the adversary will face final judgment, but we know and understand that he and the rebellious angels were cast out of heaven. God moved Satan out from His throne, that true worship would be contained in His presence.

Though the adversary still exercises power, it is not in God's presence or with His endorsement. Praise and worship leaders who follow in Lucifer's path may continue to operate in ministry, but have no endorsement of the Lord.

Worship continued in heaven. In the Old Testament, the visions of God were accompanied by the seraphims and cherubims in worship before the throne.

> *I saw also the Lord sitting upon a throne, high and lifted up, and his train filled the temple. Above it stood the seraphims: each one had six wings; with twain he covered his face, and*

with twain he covered his feet, and with twain he did fly. And one cried unto another, and said, Holy, holy, holy, is the Lord of hosts: the whole earth is full of his glory. Isaiah 6:1-3 (KJV)

However, God had a plan that worship not only continue in heaven, but also continue in the crown of His creation, man. In the next chapter, we will examine God's creation and formation of the worshiper. If we are to enter into the throne room through worship, we must understand how and why man was created.

| Chapter |
| 3 |

The Worshiper
Created

In the beginning, God created the heaven, the earth, and all living creatures. He ended the creative process by creating man in His image and likeness. From the man, He formed the woman. After His creation and placement of them in the Garden, He blessed them and commanded them.

> *And God blessed them, and God said unto them, Be fruitful, and multiply, and replenish the earth, and subdue it: and have dominion over the fish of the sea, and over the fowl of the air, and over every living thing that moveth upon the earth. Gen 1:28 (KJV)*

It is within this verse, we discover some great truths concerning worship in the life of the believer. Worship leaders and those in the congregation are responsible for these as they enter into worship.

The Worshiper Demonstrates Dominion

God intended for man to have dominion of all that was created. Regardless of the living creatures' size, gender, or habitation, the man was to have dominion. True worship of God should come from a place of dominion and give us dominion. What does this mean?

Worship is not only an expression of God's greatness, but His supremacy. Worship then is to be offered regardless of what is happening in an individual's life. If I am depressed, my worship will give me dominion over it. If I am sad, worship brings me to a place of joy. If I am confused, worship gives me dominion over it granting me peace and hope in the Lord.

> *Thou wilt shew me the path of life: in thy presence is fulness of joy; at thy right hand there are pleasures for evermore. Psalms 16:11 (KJV)*

The man was given dominion; the believer's true worship is a clear demonstration of dominion in action. With this understanding, worship will not be based upon how a person feels, but upon the power and faithfulness of God. This will give the believer dominion over every trial, test, and tribulation that can come against him or her in the world.

The Worshiper Bears Fruit

God commanded them to be fruitful. The Christian's worship is to bear fruit. It does not mean that we are to produce better songs and musicians; it means that the worship should bear fruit in the personal lives of those involved. The worship leaders and others involved should bear the fruits of worship in their character and conduct. Paul stated,

> *But we all, with open face beholding as in a glass the glory of the Lord, are changed into the same image from glory to glory, even as by the Spirit of the Lord. 2 Cor 3:18 (KJV)*

Paul wrote that as we behold God's glory, we are changed into that glory. When we enter into worship, we behold His presence, we in turn, should become transformed; that is bear fruit in our personalities.

Hence, the command to worship and be fruitful cannot be viewed individually. We are to worship Him in reverence and with holy lives. True worship not only reveals God, but our weaknesses that need to be submitted to Him. It is only through this that we can consistently have a throne room experience.

The Worshiper Multiplies

God commanded the man and woman to multiply. They were to produce others after their kind. Worship leaders and those involved in worship should produce other worshipers. This command rests heavily on those who lead praise and worship. The execution of their ministries should produce worship in others. When reading the Psalms, we discover David's devotion to the worship of God only could lead others to worship God.

However, worship leaders are not the only individuals responsible for the multiplication of worshipers. Those in the congregation of believers should also demonstrate true worship to provoke others to become worshipers of God in sincerity and truth.

The mystery of this dynamic, however, is that if one operates in a false form of worship, they can multiply the wrong type of worshipers in the church. This is where worship leaders must be careful. Man was created to reproduce after his kind. If one operates in true worship, he will produce more true worshipers. Conversely, the wrong type of worshiper will produce others of the same sort.

| Chapter 4 |

The Worshiper Prepared

Regardless on one's role in the worship setting (worship leader, singer, musician, or lay worshiper), proper preparation is necessary. Through Jesus Christ, the believer has access to the throne of God.

Having therefore, brethren, boldness to enter into the holiest by the blood of Jesus. Heb 10:19 (KJV)

Every believer, by Christ's blood, has access to the very throne room of God. However, one should not come before His presence in an unworthy manner. Hence, the worshiper should always be prepared when going before the Lord whether in prayer, praise, or worship.

How then in the worshiper prepared to enter into a throne room experience through worship? There are three ways (among many) that the worshiper is prepared to enter into true worship.

——— **Worship the Lord in the Beauty of Holiness** ———

Prepared through the Anointing

The anointing of God is His endowment of His Spirit upon an individual. Everyone that has experienced the new birth in Jesus Christ and has received the indwelling of His Spirit possesses an anointing. Remember the words of John,

> *But the anointing which ye have received of him abideth in you, and ye need not that any man teach you: but as the same anointing teacheth you of all things, and is truth, and is no lie, and even as it hath taught you, ye shall abide in him. 1 John 2:27 (KJV)*

If the Holy Spirit dwells in you, you have an anointing that abides daily. This anointing has nothing to do with an endowment for ministry and service, but an abiding presence, which brings you into God's truth, and before His throne. The Holy Spirit in you gives you proper preparation to enter into a true worship experience. In spite of this truth, many do not enter into a throne room experience. Why?: because individuals frustrate the work of the Holy Spirit in their lives.

Paul, in his writings, reveal how we frustrate the work of the Holy Spirit which causes us to negate the anointing to worship which is in all believers. We frustrate the work through grieving the Holy Spirit.

And grieve not the holy Spirit of God, whereby ye are sealed unto the day of redemption. Eph 4:30 (KJV)

We grieve the Holy Spirit through ungodly conduct. Paul wrote this exhortation when encouraging the Ephesians on how to treat one another. When worship leaders and others do not treat and interact with members of the church in godly fashion, it grieves the Spirit and hinders the corporate body from entering into God's very presence. Nevertheless, remember, you have an anointing (if the Spirit be in you) to enter into true worship.

Prepared through Suffering

No one likes to suffer. However, suffering produces brokenness, which delivers individuals from being controlled by their flesh. When the flesh is not in control, one is able to lead others in worship, and others are able to worship God in purity. The scriptures declare,

...for he that hath suffered in the flesh hath ceased from sin; That he no longer should live the rest of his time in the flesh to the lusts of men, but to the will of God. 1 Peter 4:1-2 (KJV)

Suffering aids in the believer forsaking sin and no longer living to please the flesh. Suffering's perfect work is revealed in power and passionate worship. The scriptures reveal also that Jesus learned obedience through the things that He suffered.

> *Though he were a Son, yet learned he obedience by the things which he suffered. Heb 5:8 (KJV)*

If Christ learned obedience, the believer learns true obedience through the sufferings, which God allows. In turn, the believer will offer true worship to Christ. Suffering will prepare the believer for a throne room experience.

Prepared through Character

We stated in the last chapter that man was created to bear fruit. The Christian is to bear fruit in relationship to their worship. The bearing of fruit is reflected in the Christian's character. As previously stated, we should exhibit the fruit of the Spirit as outlined in the letter to the Galatians,

> *But, the fruit of the Spirit is love, joy, peace, longsuffering, gentleness, goodness, faith, Meekness, temperance: against such there is no law. Gal 5:22-23 (KJV)*

At the beginning of the list of the fruit of the Spirit is love. The worshiper must be governed by compassion. Our motivation, even in worship, should be to demonstrate God's love. The Word declares that the world will know that we are Jesus' disciples by the love that we display one for another. God is love and we are to represent His love (I John 4:8).

The next fruit listed is joy. Happiness is dependent upon events and "happenings" in life. Joy can be present even in adverse situations. Trials and tests are a part of the kingdom experience. As we wait upon the Lord, God wants us to experience joy in our walk with Him and in worship. Paul stated that the Kingdom of God is righteousness, joy, and peace in the Holy Ghost (Romans 14:7).

We all want peace. It is listed next as one of the fruit. Even when the world falls apart around us, the peace of God will guard our hearts and minds. If we do not develop any other fruit of the Spirit, we should seek for peace and let God's peace dwell in us in adverse situations (John 14:27). After peace, Paul adds patience. Everyone could use more patience. We must be able to endure and wait on God (Isaiah 40:31).

In order to reflect the nature of a loving God, kindness must also be developed. We must be kind to all, displaying the love of the Father. He is our ultimate example of kindness (Luke 6:35).

Next, we must allow goodness to dwell in us. We should strive to display good unto all men, in spite of their actions, in and outside of the Church (Galatians 6:10). God is faithful to us, even when we lose our hope and faith. This is why the fruit of faithfulness has to be present. Faithfulness always has a reward. Let us be like God. He is always faithful (I Corinthians 4:2).

Then, gentleness must be achieved. We must not deal with people out of a harsh spirit (especially the worship leader), but from one of care and concern (Galatians 6:1). When we are wrong, we desire mercy. The believer should offer this same courtesy towards others.

Most important, Christians need self-control. If we have control over our thoughts and actions, we become candidates for true worship. We must not only practice self-control when it comes to the flesh, but also in our dealings with others (James 3:2). God commanded them to be fruitful. With these in place, the believer is prepared to enter into worship.

In the next chapters, we will turn our attention to the worship leader in particular. Though all participate in worship, not all are set aside to lead others into worship. Therefore, it is important that those who lead worship and/or have a desire to do so be fully prepared to do so with the proper motives, character, and understanding. The truths presented will also help those who participate in worship.

| Chapter 5 |

The Tools of Worship

Those involved in worship ministry have to be prepared. The proper tools are necessary is one is to lead others into worship. Some believe that the main tools for leading others into worship are skill and abilities. However, these things are secondary.

A true worship leader will be known primarily by his or understanding of the Lord and His ways and secondarily by their musical abilities. The primary tools for true worship are founded upon understanding.

Wisdom is the principal thing; therefore get wisdom: and with all thy getting get understanding Prov 4:7 (KJV)

Proverbs declares that wisdom is first, but you need understanding with all the wisdom that is acquired. This holds true for the worship leader. Gain all the skill and knowledge in music, singing, etc., but have an understanding. The worship leader should have a full understanding of three areas, if they will lead others.

Understanding the Object of Worship

What is the object of the Christian's worship? Do we participate in praise and worship to move the service along? Is worship designed to make us seem pious or reverent? Do we participate in worship for the sake of worship? The one who leads worship must understand the object (focus, center, or subject) of worship. The object of worship is God and the Lord Jesus Christ.

The above statement seems obvious; however, this is not what is seen demonstrated in some churches. Worship finds in definition in the nature and character of God. Worship comes as a response to the greatness of God and salvation provided through Jesus Christ.

If the worship leader is not careful, worship itself can become the object of worship rather than God. Worship begins with the revelation of God's greatness and ends with appreciation for what He has done in our lives. The worship leader is responsible to bring people face to face with God.

A worship leader who forgets to lead people to the true object of worship inadvertently leads the people into idolatry.

Thou shalt not make unto thee any graven image, or any likeness of anything that is in heaven above, or that is in the earth beneath, or that is in the water under the earth:5 Thou shalt not bow down thyself to them, nor serve them: for I the Lord thy God am a jealous God...Ex 20:4-5 (KJV)

God has to be the center and reason for worship. When worship is directed toward any other person, place, or thing aside from God, it becomes false and idol worship. The response of people cannot be the object of worship. Moreover, worship should not be seen as a space-filler in a service. This is false worship. Worship has to be offered in direct response to God's supremacy, mercy, and excellent works towards His people.

Understanding the Objective of Worship

The worship leader must understand what is the objective or goal of worship. We have already stated that it cannot be to move a service along or evoke an emotional response from those in the church. Preparing the hearts of people to receive the Word of God cannot be the objective of worship; though it is a beneficial by-product. There is a three-fold objective to worship that the worship leader must keep in view.

Declare God's Glory & Nature

One of the primary objectives of worship is to declare God's glory and divine nature. When we look again at Isaiah's description of God's throne, we find the angels declaring,

And one cried unto another, and said, Holy, holy, holy, is the Lord of hosts: the whole earth is full of his glory. Isaiah 6:3 (KJV)

The angels declared God's holiness and his glory (works, power, and acts) in the earth. When we enter into worship, our goal should be to declare who and how our God is. The worship leader who has this in mind will choose songs, which point to God's greatness and not man's plight. The worship leader will bring others into a place where God's nature and power is exalted above man's experiences. In doing so, they will lead others into the very throne room of God.

Demonstrating Submission & Expressing Appreciation

Worship involves the exaltation of one and the submission of another. The second core objective of worship is to demonstrate our submission and obedience to God. We declare that He is our creator and we are submitted to Him through our worship.

O come, let us worship and bow down: let us kneel before the Lord our maker. Psalms 95:6 (KJV)

The worship leader must have this in mind as he or she leads others. Whenever God is exalted, access to His presence is unrestricted.

My praise shall be of thee in the great congregation: I will pay my vows before them that fear him. Psalms 22:25 (KJV)

——— **Worship the Lord in the Beauty of Holiness** ———

The psalmist understood that it was his responsibility as a servant of God to praise Him and pay his vows. It was a sign of submission and reverence. Sometimes we can be caught up in the hype of the people being uplifted by the worship. It is important to remain humble knowing that it is all about God. The worship leader job is to help bring others in the congregation to place of submission through worship. When this occurs, God presence is made manifest cause He makes His abode with the humble.

The third core objective of worship is appreciation. Appreciation should produce worship as well as praise.

> *I will worship toward thy holy temple, and praise thy name for thy lovingkindness and for thy truth: for thou hast magnified thy word above all thy name Psalms 138:2 (KJV)*

The psalmist stated that he would worship and praise in appreciation for God's loving-kindness and truth. The worship leader must be mindful that grateful worship leads to great worship in His presence.

Understanding the Obstacles of Worship

Many obstacles to worship exist. The worship leader must recognize external and internal obstacles that hinder worship and their ability to bring others into the throne room. Three main obstacles hinder the worship leader as they strive to lead others.

1) **Wrong Motives** – The worship leader must be honest about personal motives, agendas and insecurities, else true worship is unattainable. The worship leader cannot be motivated by praise, money, or success.

Worship leaders have to be on guard not to forget the purpose of worship. They have to avoid being wrapped up in the quality of the production (lights, camera, and action) and drawing more attention to themselves rather than the quality of the worship.

Worship leaders cannot use success in worship ministry to fill personal desires for acceptance and appreciation. These things become obstacles to leading others into the presence of the Lord.

2) **Wrong Environment** – The setting or environment may be an obstacle. We are not speaking of location, but of the mindset of the congregation or group as a whole. The worship leader has to be sensitive to the environment, even in church.

There could be many reasons why the worship environment may seem dry, dead, or not conducive to worship. When this occurs, the worship leader has to know how to bring the people into a place where God can be worshiped properly.

This cannot be done through criticizing or fussing at the congregants. You cannot get a spiritual response from the people by a fleshly admonition.

3) **Wrong Spirit** – We are specifically referring to spiritual warfare. The scriptures are clear that not every spirit is of God.

Beloved, believe not every spirit, but try the spirits whether they are of God.1 John 4:1 (KJV)

A wrong spirit may show up to hinder the worship of God. The worship leader should know how to engage in spiritual warfare to allow true worship to go forwards.

Other hindrances and obstacles exist; yet, the above three represent those frequently faced by the worship leader. If the worship leader remains mindful, prayerful, and full of the Spirit, these obstacles will pose little threat to the successful worship of God.

|Chapter 6|

The Tendons of Worship

The title of this chapter brings definition to the role of the worship leader. In the human body, tendons are intricate to the body's movement and functioning.

Tendon - a tough cord or band of dense white fibrous connective tissue that unites a muscle with some other part (as a bone) and transmits the force, which the muscle exerts.

The worship leader acts as a tendon between the presence of God and the people of God. The same way a natural tendon transmits the force of the muscle, the worship leader brings others into the Spirit, which proceeds from God. Hence, worship leaders act as the tendons of worship. The worship leader must understand that as a tendon, they must lead others. The leadership of those involved in worship is three-fold.

Lead by Influence not Manipulation

Worship leaders must learn to lead by influence and not manipulation. Influence and manipulation are polar opposites.

Influence - the capacity or power of persons or things to be a compelling force on or produced effects on the action, behavior of others

Manipulation - exerting shrewd or devious influences especially for one's own advantage, getting what you want by ignoring or harming others'

Worship leaders have influence. Influence is given to lead others to God. Influence has to be used to bring people to the object of worship. The authority and influence the worship leader possesses is designed to give them what they need to brings others before the throne of God in true worship. However, the opposite happens at times.

When the worship leaders are not prepared, not godly, or not focused, they may fall into relying on manipulation. Manipulation is a selfish force, which will cause people to focus on the worship leader rather than on God. Manipulation will cause the worship leader to walk in the way of Lucifer. They will desire worship for themselves and their musical abilities. The worship leader must remember that worship should always be about getting the people what they need (from God) and getting them to a place where they understand real worship.

Lead by Lifestyle not Language

Talk is cheap. A worship leader leads others into worship by living a life of worship. In the first chapter, we stated that the believer is to be worship.

The worship leader cannot have the language of worship without the lifestyle. When this occurs, their worship ministry is ineffective, ungodly, and will lead others away from the presence of God.

Earlier we spoke of spiritual warfare as an obstacle. Satan understands the importance for man to be in the presence of God and endeavor to stop people from entering in. The worship leader who does not lead by lifestyle leaves vulnerability for the adversary to distract him or her from their purpose.

Because worship leaders play a role in the direction of a service, the adversary looks for an opening in their lives to affect those who will be exposed to their ministry and service. A pure lifestyle shuts the door for the adversary using the worship leader in an ungodly manner in the church service.

The role of worship leaders can be extremely detrimental to themselves and to everyone who trusts them to lead them into the presence of God. Worship leaders have to approach the throne room with the right heart! If not this could produce God's displeasure with what is accepted. God did not receive Cain's offering and He will not receive our offering of worship if it is tainted.

Lead to the Place You've Been

Everybody cannot and should not lead others in worship. The worship leader should find it easy to lead others into the presence of the Lord. Why? They should know they way to His presence based upon their daily living. The lifestyle of a worship leader places them in a position to lead others. Hence, the worship leader should make sure they meet spiritual qualifications to bring others into God's presence. Let us now look at more closely the lifestyle requirements of a true worship leader:

1) The worship leader must first know the way into His presence. (How can you lead others somewhere you have never been or do not have access to?) The Spirit searches the deep things of God.

   > *But God hath revealed them unto us by his Spirit: for the Spirit searcheth all things, yea, the deep things of God. 1 Cor 2:10 (KJV)*

2) Again, worship must be a lifestyle for the worship leader. (Worship is not something we do it is a lifestyle). The worship leader walks in the Spirit.

   > *If we live in the Spirit, let us also walk in the Spirit. Gal 5:25 (KJV)*

3) The worship leader must know how to operate in the Spirit. (The worship leader should understand spiritual truths and spiritual gifts). He or she should not be ignorant in this area.

   > *Now concerning spiritual gifts, brethren, I would not have you ignorant. 1 Cor 12:1 (KJV)*

4) The worship leader must be prophetic (Has nothing to do with the prophetic office, but understand the voice of God and understand the move of God) **

5) The worship leader must have and be led the Spirit of God.

   For as many as are led by the Spirit of God, they are the sons of God. Romans 8:14 (KJV)

6) The worship leader must know how to set order. (God cannot operate in a place where there is no order).

   Let all things be done decently and in order. 1 Cor 14:40 (KJV)

** The reason why worship leaders have to be prophetic is that they have to be able to discern the mind of God for a particular setting. In doing so, the worship leader will be able to facilitate what God wants to do and be a conduit for what the people while in His presence. **

The worship leader has an important place in the worship service. He or she must remember that the quality of their leadership is important to the name of Christ being exalted and God's purpose being accomplished in the worship setting.

<table>
<tr><td>Chapter
7</td></tr>
</table>

The Throne Room Experience

What really is the throne room experience? Is it what happens in the powerful worship service? Or is it something else? The throne room experience begins with the worship setting where we are in God's presence, experiencing His glory and power. However, the result of the throne room experience is a lifestyle characterized by worship. In the final chapter, we want to look at the results of the prepared worship leader and worshiper entering into God's presence, beholding His glory.

Worship in Action

The throne room experience produces worship in action in the life of the believer. In the daily life of the believer, a throne will experience will cause the believer to:

Bow/Prostrate to His Standards for Living

> ***O worship the Lord in the beauty of holiness: fear before him, all the earth. (Psalm 69:9)***

In this verse, worship means to bow and prostrate before the Lord. In everyday life, the believer will worship God as He submits to His standards for living. The throne room experience produces daily worship as we bow to His commands.

> *For the grace of God that bringeth salvation hath appeared to all men, Teaching us that, denying and worldly lusts, we should live soberly, righteously, and godly, in this present world. (Titus 2:11-12)*

Our reception of God's grace teaches us that true worship manifests in separation and sanctification. When we do this in our lives, we are bowing our lives in worship of Him.

Swim in (Live in) His Presence

> *Exalt ye the Lord our God, and worship at his footstool; for he is holy. (Psalm 99:5)*

The word translated worship here means a pond to swim in. The psalmist is calling the people to exalt God and swim in (at) His footstool. We do this as a result of the throne room experience. We all will walk in the Spirit daily.

> *If we live in the Spirit, let us also walk in the Spirit. (Galatians 5:25)*

Walking by the Spirit constitutes worship. As we allow the Spirit to lead us daily, we worship God. The only way one is able to swim is there is an abundance of water. As we are filled daily with the

Holy Spirit and submit to His unction, we are in worship.

Serve the Lord in Ministry and Good Works

> **But this I confess unto thee, that after the way which they call heresy, so worship I the God of my fathers, believing all things which are written in the law and in the prophets. (Acts 24:14)**

In his defense of the gospel, Paul stated that he worshipped the God of Israel. The word he used for worship denoted religious service. He described worship of God by faithfully ministering and serving for Him and in His name.

Thus, the throne room experience will inspire worship of God through passionate witnessing in His name and perform good works, which includes organized religious service.

> **Let your light so shine before men, that they may see your good works, and glorify your Father, which is in heaven. (Matthew 5:16)**

God receives glory when we perform good works. Good works are an outward of an inner relationship. The Throne room experience ensures they are done with the right motives, reflecting our daily worship of God through them. When we serve in the Church, do volunteer work, and the like, we worship God through our actions.

Worship the Lord in the Beauty of Holiness

The throne room experience produces true worship developed from reverence and awe of God's authority, majesty, and greatness. Worship sets God on the throne and places us at His feet. When we walk in worship, we walk in the fear of the Lord. Our fear is born out of respect for who He is. His supremacy is seen and felt throughout all creation.

> *Serve the Lord with fear, and rejoice with trembling. (Psalm 2:11)*

If one does not respect, fear, and reverence God, the worship offered is a religious exercise only. A throne room experience will eradicate meaningless worship experiences. It will produce worship that is acceptable unto God, which transcends the religious setting and permeates through everyday living. When we offer this type of worship, God is exalted and we will be transformed in His presence (in or outside of the church setting).

Worship in Acronym (W.O.R.S.H.I.P.)

To conclude our discussion of worship, we have developed an acronym for worship to help further bring definition to the dynamics of true worship. The throne room experience will produce these dynamics in the worship of God.

W – Worship provides a **WAY** into the presence of God. One has to have a **WILL** to seek Him. (Psalms 27:4, Matt 9:20)

O - Worship sets **ORDER** in the service. Worship charges the atmosphere to become conducive and submissive to the will of the Holy Ghost. (I Corinthians 14:40, John 4:21-24)

R – Worship prepares the heart to receive **REVELATION**, causing hidden things to be revealed, and things not previously noted to be acknowledged or confronted by the Spirit of God. We communicate to God through our prayer and worship. God speaks to us and about things concerning us through our worshipping him. Therefore, during prayer, as on enters into worship, answers are received.

S – Worship cause natural and spiritual **SHIFTS** in our lives. When we begin to worship a transformation unseen takes place. The manifestation thereof is the dissolution of the very thing that attempted to overtake the people of God. When we change our posture from standing in pride to bowing in humility, God will move on our behalf. The victory is ours, yet the glory is God's! (Acts 16:25)

H – True worship is characterized by **HUMILITY**. Worship begins with submission and appreciation. Humility will cause believers to be thankful in worship and not motivated by what they can receive only. (Psalm 100:4)

I – Worship is only a religious act without intimacy. **INTIMACY** brings fellowship and communion with God. Once you enter the throne room, the real exchange happens. (Matt 26:7, Mark 14:3, Luke 7:37-47)

P – Worship involves **PARTICIPATION**. Worship in demonstrated with physical activities such as singing, lifting of hands, bowing of heads, bending of knees and laying prostrate.

We should count it an honor to be able to draw near to God in worship. Those who lead worship should regard it as a double honor. Remember, the throne room experience leads to the worship of God being executed in the daily life of the believer. We declare again, "The throne room experience begins with the worship setting where we are in God's presence, experiencing His glory and power. However, the result of the throne room experience is a lifestyle characterized by worship."

ABOUT CALVIN L. LEWIS

Book author, motivational speaker, conference director, and playwright are a few of the creative hats arrayed by Calvin L. Lewis. Possessing a vast pool of creative ingenuity, this "dream chaser" is a man after God's own heart and has a heart for people.

Lewis, the founder and executive director of Dream Chasers Worldwide, Inc. (DCW), an organization created to assist people live their best lives and reach their highest potential and as the visionary founder of another spiritually uplifting and up building effort, Remnant House Inc, a ministry fostering the spiritual reconciliation of those that have been spurned by the "traditional church" and victims of "church hurt" Lewis' aim is to mirror the life and teachings of Christ to a hurting world.

As a writer his first published book, 'The Birthing of a Vision' is filled with a message of hope, love, inspiration, and spiritual tools to aid its reader to victorious living. Extending his Christian faith and creative astuteness to the stage Lewis wrote, produced, and directed his debut stage play the 'The Gift' in 2007 and is developing his sophomore production 'The Power of a Praying Woman' that premiered February 13, 2010.

"I believe that inspiring and motivating others pleases God and it allows Him to move me closer to my destiny, my moment of excellence. Living life to my fullest potential honors God and that is my goal, says Lewis in regard to being known as a "dream chaser." Lewis is a South Georgia native he is available for workshops, seminars, worship services, and book signings.

——— **Worship the Lord in the Beauty of Holiness** ———

ABOUT RODERICK L. EVANS

Roderick L. Evans is a solid voice in the Christian community. He has a three-fold ministry as minister, author, and publisher; writing numerous books, articles, blogs, teaching resources, devotional materials, and music for the Christian community.

Roderick L. Evans is the founder of Kingdom Builders International Ministries. A ministry dedicated to promoting maturity, unity, and holiness in the Body of Christ.

He is also the founder of Ananias Men's Fellowship, a ministry offering resources for the enrichment and edification of Christian men everywhere. In addition, he is the founder of Kingdom Builders Publishing, Kingdom Builders Productions, and Asaph Music.

He is the author of two popular blogs, "According to Roderick…" and "Manna Moments with Roderick L. Evans," which provide relevant spiritual insights through biblical inspiration. Recognized nationally and internationally as a prophetic voice, his preaching and teaching ministry is recognized as foundational, inspirational, and prophetical. His messages have been known to transform lives and encourage members of the Christian faith.

He, his wife Letitia, and their son Seth reside in Elizabeth City, North Carolina, from which he travels ministering the word of the Lord.

www.ingramcontent.com/pod-product-compliance
Lightning Source LLC
LaVergne TN
LVHW091210080426
835509LV00006B/918